LIFE IN THE
DESERTS

Author: **Lucy Baker**

Consultant: Roger Hammond,
Director of Living Earth

PRINCETON ■ LONDON

Created by
act-two Ltd

Published in the United States and Canada by
Two-Can Publishing LLC
234 Nassau Street
Princeton, NJ 08542

For information on other Two-Can books and multimedia,
Call 1-609-921-6700, fax 1-609-921-3349, or visit our web site at
http;//www.two-canpublishing.com

ISBN: 1-58728-567-3 (SC)
ISBN: 1-58728-552-5 (HC)

2 4 6 8 10 9 7 5 3

Printed in Hong Kong

Photographic Credits:
p.4 (left) Heather Angel/Biofotos (right) NHPA p.5 Biofotos/Brian Rogers p.7 Ardea/François Gohier p.8 (left) Ardea/François Gohier (right) Bruce Coleman
p.9 Ardea p.10 (top) ZEFA/Klaus Hachenberg (bottom) Bruce Coleman/Carol Hughes p.11 (top) Ardea/K.W. Fink (bottom) Ardea/François Gohier p.12-13
Ardea/Clem Haagner p.14 Planet Earth/Hans Christian Heap p.15 Science Photo Library/Keith Kent p.16 (top) Ardea/Peter Steyn (bottom) The Hutchison
Library p.17 ZEFA/J. Bitsch p.18 (top) B. & C. Alexander (bottom) ZEFA/R. Steedman p.19 Impact Photos/David Reed p.20-21 Mark Edwards p.22
Oxfam/Jeremy Hartley p.23 (top) Picturepoint (bottom) Impact Photos/David Reed p.31 B. & C. Alexander
Front cover: NHPA/Anthony Bannister. Back cover: Ardea/Clem Haagner

Illustrations by Francis Mosley. Story illustrated by Valerie McBride.

CONTENTS

LOOKING AT THE DESERTS

There are places where rain hardly ever falls and few plants can survive, where the sun scorches the earth and strong winds whip sand and dust from the ground. These places are called **deserts**. But not all deserts are areas of shifting sands and intense heat. In fact, rock and gravel cover the greater part of most deserts. Some deserts, such as the Gobi Desert in Asia, are actually cold for most of the year. Other deserts are blisteringly hot during the day, but temperatures drop dramatically during the night.

A surprising variety of plant and animal life struggles to survive the harsh conditions of the desert, and many people call it their home.

DID YOU KNOW?

The scientific definition of a desert is "a place that has very little vegetation and receives less than 10 inches (25 centimeters) of rain each year." This means that the land mass at the South Pole could be called a desert, because it receives only a few inches (centimeters) of rain each year. The water does not fall as rain, however, but snow!

▶ Some of the highest sand dunes in the world can be found in the Namib Desert in southern Africa. Sand dunes are not fixed features of the desert. They are mobile mounds of sand that are shaped by the wind.

▼ Death Valley, California, is the hottest, driest area of the United States.

▼ A boulder-strewn part of the Namib Desert shows signs of life after a good year's rainfall.

WHERE IN THE WORLD?

Deserts cover about one-fifth of all the land in the world. There are deserts in parts of Africa, Asia, Australia, and North and South America.

Most deserts lie along two imaginary lines north and south of the equator, called the **Tropic of Cancer** and the **Tropic of Capricorn**. Here, and in other desert regions, dry air currents blow across the land. These dry air currents can blow hot or cold, but they rarely carry rain clouds. Consequently the lands they cross are starved of rain and given no protection from the sun.

This map shows the main desert areas of the world. Do you live near desert lands?

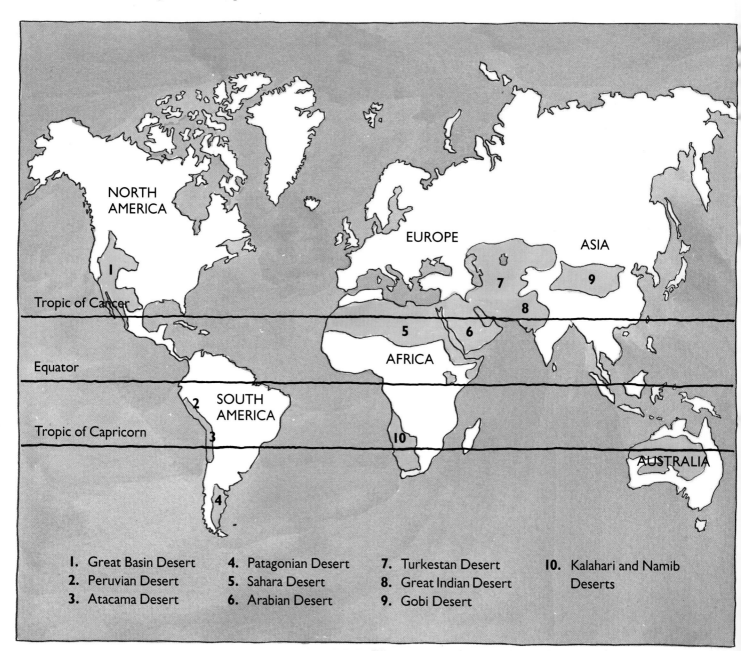

1. Great Basin Desert
2. Peruvian Desert
3. Atacama Desert
4. Patagonian Desert
5. Sahara Desert
6. Arabian Desert
7. Turkestan Desert
8. Great Indian Desert
9. Gobi Desert
10. Kalahari and Namib Deserts

RAIN SHADOWS

Some deserts are called rain shadow deserts. These occur where large mountains block the path of rain-bearing wind. The raised mountain ground pushes the wind upward and as it rises, it cools. The drop in temperature causes clouds carried by the wind to burst and release their rain. The wind continues over the mountains, but by the time it reaches the other side it carries no rain clouds. This natural process creates some of the world's wettest environments—rain forests—alongside the world's driest.

● The Sahara in northern Africa is the largest desert in the world. It covers an area roughly the size of the United States.

● The Gobi Desert in eastern Asia is situated on high, windy plains. It is the coldest desert in the world.

● Nearly half of Australia is covered by desert.

● The Arabian Desert is the sandiest desert in the world.

● The smallest desert regions of the world are the Peruvian and Atacama deserts on the western coast of South America.

● Many of the world's deserts are bordered by areas of scant vegetation. These **scrublands** would become true deserts if they were to lose their native trees and plants.

▲ Ancient rock paintings in African and Asian deserts show giraffes, antelope, and other grazing animals that could not survive in today's desert conditions. This suggests that the lands were once more **fertile**. Evidence of ancient lakes and forests can also be found in the world's deserts.

DESERT PLANTS

It is astonishing that any plants have learned to survive in desert conditions. Most plants rely on regular rainfall, but desert plants may have to go without fresh water for more than a year. In addition, many desert plants have to cope with both hot and cold temperatures, as each boiling day turns into another freezing night.

Some desert plants remain hidden in the ground as seeds until rain falls. By waiting until conditions are good, they do not have to cope with the rigors of desert life.

▼ The gigantic welwitschia plant is unique to the Namib Desert. This desert has a rare water source—fogs that drift across it from the coast. The welwitschia's leaves absorb tiny particles of water from the foggy air.

▲ Cacti are the most famous desert plants. They are native to North and South American deserts, but they have been introduced to other parts of the world.

Prickly pear cacti were taken to Australia and planted as hedges around homes in the outback. They grew so quickly that large areas were overrun by the spiky plants. Small creatures that eat the prickly pear's soft insides had to be introduced to Australia to help reclaim the land.

▶ Cacti are flowering plants. Some cacti produce flowers every year, while others rarely come into blossom. Birds visit cacti to extract sugary nectar from their flowers or search their stems for insects.

The cactus in this picture is a giant saguaro. Saguaro cacti can grow to nearly 50 feet (15 meters) in height and may hold several tons (kilograms) of water in their swollen stems. Like other cacti, the saguaro has no leaves. Instead, prickly spines grow around its stem. These spines create a layer of still air around the surface of the plant and so protect it from drying winds.

SURVIVAL TRICKS

Desert plants have special ways of surviving without regular rainfall. Some suck up as much water as they can during occasional rains and then store it in their stems or leaves. Here are some other ways desert plants collect and conserve water.

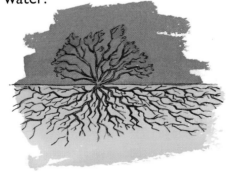

Some desert trees have long **taproots**, which grow deep into the ground to reach underground water sources.

Many plants, like the creosote bush, have a vast network of shallow roots to extract every available drop of moisture from their patch of the desert.

Some desert plants store food and water underground in thickened roots, bulbs, or **tubers**. The stems of such plants, exposed to sun and wind, may look dead, but as soon as it rains they spring into life, producing leaves, fruits, and flowers.

HIDDEN LIFE

It is difficult to believe that hundreds of different animals live in deserts. Most of the time, these are quiet, still places. This is because many desert creatures move around only at dawn or dusk. At other times of the day, they burrow underground or hide beneath rocks or plants to avoid very hot or cold conditions.

The animals living in the desert rely on plant life and on each other for their survival. Roots, stems, leaves, and seeds form the basic diet of many desert creatures, and they, in turn, are hunted by other animals. The largest hunters in the desert include wild cats, foxes, and wolves.

Some desert creatures get all the water they need from the food they eat. Others have to travel long distances to visit rare water holes.

▲ Scorpions hunt spiders, insects, and other small animals on the desert floor. Once they have caught their meal, they use the poisonous stings at the end of their tails to kill their prey. People stung by a scorpion usually suffer just a sharp pain, but the most powerful scorpion stings can be deadly.

▼ Many reptiles are successful desert dwellers, especially snakes and lizards. Some snakes have a special way of moving across shifting sands. They throw their heads to one side and their bodies follow in a loop. This is called sidewinding. Snakes can also burrow into the sand to cool down or escape from predators.

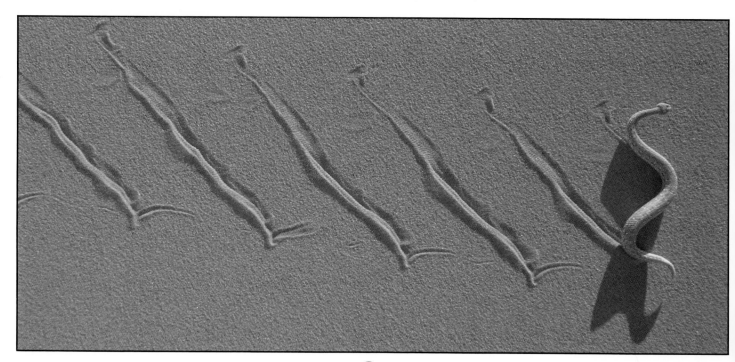

▶ Rabbits, gerbils, and many other small mammals live in desert lands. The cottontail rabbit, right, can be found in some American deserts. It has large ears that act as radiators, giving off heat and so helping the rabbit to cool down.

▼ Many lizards live in the world's deserts. Like other reptiles, they have a scaly skin that stops them from drying up in the baking sunshine. Most lizards are insect-eaters. They chase flies or sit patiently waiting for a beetle or a line of ants to pass them by. Lizards have many enemies, so they must stay on their guard. The horned lizard, below, has excellent camouflage that makes it hard to find on the desert floor.

CROSSING THE DESERT

The largest desert animals do not remain in one area of the desert. They travel long distances in search of food and water. Small numbers of antelope, goats, and sheep are found in most deserts of the world. A rare horse, called Przewalski's horse, once roamed the cold Gobi Desert but is now thought to be **extinct** in the wild.

The most famous animal to cross the desert is the camel. The camel is sometimes called the ship of the desert, because it can travel over vast seas of inhospitable rock and sand better than any other animal.

There are two kinds of camels. The dromedary has one hump on its back and a thin coat. It is native to the hot deserts of Arabia and North Africa, but it also has been introduced to parts of America and Australia. The Bactrian camel has two humps and a darker, thicker coat than its cousin. It comes from the cooler central Asian deserts.

Camels are well built for desert life. They have bushy eyebrows and two rows of eyelashes to help keep the sand out of their eyes. Their slit nostrils can be closed for the same reason. Their two-toed feet spread out as they walk and stop them from sinking into the sand.

The humps on camels' backs do not contain water as was once believed. They hold fat reserves that can be broken down into food when camels are crossing the desert. If a camel is starving, its hump will shrink.

DID YOU KNOW?

● Less than 100 years ago, it was impossible to cross the vast Sahara and Arabian deserts without the help of a camel. Today cars and trucks are used for many desert journeys, and camels are becoming less important to the lives of desert people.

● Thirsty camels can drink up to 30 gallons (140 liters) of water in one sitting and then go for more than a week without water.

● Camels are the domestic animals of the desert. They are used as transportation. They provide meat and milk for food. Their hairy coats are woven into cloth. Even the camel's dry droppings are used as fuel for cooking fires.

WHEN WATER FALLS

Some deserts have regular rainy seasons, but others may not see rain for many years. In the desert there are only torrential downpours. Violent desert rainstorms cause flash floods and destruction. Plants are washed away, and some animals drown.

Rain brings life as well as death to desert lands. Days after a heavy storm, billions of tiny seeds spring to life on the desert floor. These small flowering plants, called **ephemerals**, have been hiding in the sand since the last rainfall. Millions of insect eggs are also brought to life by the drumming rain, and so an army of flies, bees, and wasps appears. These insects feed on the ephemerals and help them to reproduce by spreading pollen from flower to flower.

Eight weeks after the rain, the desert is empty again. The colorful flowers and buzzing insects have gone. But millions and billions of new seeds and eggs now lie hidden in the desert sands. Many of them will be eaten by permanent desert dwellers, but some are bound to survive until the next rain comes and the life cycle can be repeated.

▶ Lightning strikes as a storm passes over the Sonoran Desert in North America. A whole year's rainfall can come in one single cloudburst.

▲ Colorful, flowering plants brighten the sandy Arabian Desert after a recent rainfall.

DID YOU KNOW?

● Sometimes rainstorms fail to wet the desert floor. If it is very hot when a storm occurs, the rain may turn into vapor before it reaches the ground. More than 12 inches (30 centimeters) of rain may fall during one heavy storm in the desert.

● The Atacama Desert is the driest in the world. Some parts of it experienced a 400-year drought until 1971.

DESERT PEOPLE

The desert is a dangerous place for people not used to its hostile conditions. Even so, a few people call the open desert home.

The **Bushmen** of the Kalahari Desert in southern Africa are **nomads**, which means that they travel from place to place. Bushmen survive by hunting wild game and gathering edible plants and insects. Some Aborigines once lived this way in the heart of Australia's desert lands, but most are now settled in goverment-funded camps.

The world's most barren deserts such as the Sahara, Arabian, and Gobi deserts do not have enough native plants and animals to support **hunter-gatherers**. Instead, the nomadic people take from the desert what they can but also kill or trade animals such as goats, sheep, or camels for food.

PEOPLE FACTS

Bushmen rarely drink. They get most of the water they need from plant roots and desert melons found on or under the desert floor.

The turban worn by many desert people is not a hat. It is a very long piece of cloth that is wrapped around and around the head. It helps to keep desert sand out of the eyes, nose, and mouth.

People in the cold Gobi Desert live in sturdy, round huts called yurts. These simple homes can withstand winds up to 90 miles (145 kilometers) an hour.

▶ These men belong to a group of people called the Tuareg. The Tuareg were once known as the pirates of the desert. For many years they controlled trade across the Sahara by patrolling the desert on racing camels.

◀ A Bushman of the Kalahari makes a fire by rubbing two sticks together. Bushmen have their own special language that includes clicking sounds. Bushmen live in huts built from local materials. The frame is made of branches, and the roof is thatched with long grass.

▼ Many desert nomads live in tents, like the one in this picture. When it is time to move on, the nomads pack up the tent. It is then carried by a camel or donkey.

DESERT OASES

In parts of the desert, plants grow in abundance and water is available throughout the year. These places are called oases.

Most oases are fed by underground pools of water that formed over thousands of years. The water is trapped between layers of rock below the desert floor. Rivers also create oases. The largest oasis in the world lies along the banks of the great River Nile, which flows through the Sahara.

Oases are the most densely populated areas of the desert. The regular water supply makes it possible for people to settle permanently and build villages, towns, or cities. The land is **irrigated**, and date palms, olives, wheat, millet, and other food crops are grown.

▲ If seasonal rains fail, water must be carried to the fields to keep desert crops alive.

Many desert towns are built from materials of the desert itself. Mud is mixed with straw and water to make bricks, which are then baked in the sun. This village is the home of the Dogon. Dogon people get their water from nearby mountain pools. The Dogons live in Mali, which is in northern Africa.

Oases are like green islands surrounded by a sea of sand and rock. Animals and people alike depend on oases for their drinking water.

Oases do not last forever. The world's deserts are littered with ghost towns, where the water has run dry or the oasis has been swamped by shifting sand dunes. In such places the people have moved on.

CREEPING DESERTS

The world's deserts are growing. Through a process known as **desertification**, scrub and grasslands become as dry and barren as the deserts they border. At the present rate of desertification, more than 77,220 square miles (200,000 square kilometers) of new desert land throughout the world are created every year.

Deserts naturally shrink and grow depending on the amount of rain they receive. In recent years, however, widespread droughts have caused deserts to grow at an alarming rate.

Scientists believe the droughts are part of a worldwide change in weather patterns caused by pollution in the atmosphere.

Desert nomads speed up the process of desertification by cutting down trees and grazing their animals on threatened grasslands. This leaves the land exposed to sun, wind, and occasional violent rains. The delicate **topsoil** dries out then is blown and washed away.

Intensive farming can also cause desertification. The pressure to grow

more and more food on the same amount of land encourages farmers to overwork the soil, and this can have disastrous consequences. In the 1930's, intensive farming and grazing in America's southern states created a huge area of bare and desertlike land called the Dust Bowl. Droughts had dried up the soil, and winds then carried it away. Cities hundreds of miles away were plunged into darkness as huge clouds of dust blew across the sky.

▼ If the ground cover is removed from dry scrublands, the hot sun bakes the earth. Rains run straight off the hard ground, and any remaining trees weaken and die.

DID YOU KNOW?

More than 400 million short tons (363 million metric tons) of African soil is blown west over the Atlantic Ocean every year. In 1988 hundreds of tiny, pink Saharan frogs rained down on a British village during a bad storm.

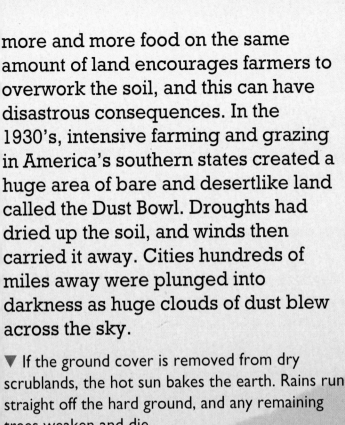

DESERTS TODAY

For centuries the world's deserts were regarded as terrifying wastelands. They remained the exclusive property of small desert tribes who managed to survive in hostile conditions. Only recently has the arrival of cars, trucks, and airplanes expanded the possibilities for desert exploration.

Today industries are active in the desert. Mining companies use massive machinery to extract rich mineral reserves such as copper, iron, salt, and uranium. Oil is also found in some deserts and has brought great wealth to certain areas. Saudi Arabia holds some of the world's largest oil fields.

Elsewhere, modern technology has been used to turn the desert green. By finding new underground water sources or by tapping nearby rivers, people can grow crops on desert lands.

Desertification is a problem in many areas of the world, but Africa is the most obvious victim. In some African countries, crops have failed for several years running, which has caused widespread **famine**. Many nomads have cast off their ancient ways of life, as lengthy droughts have left the desert bare.

◄ As rich countries transform their deserts into farmland, poorer African countries try to hold back the creeping edge of the Sahara. This man is building simple rock walls to prevent the seasonal rains from running straight off the hard ground.

DID YOU KNOW?

● In some countries, more water is used for irrigation than for any other purpose. Irrigation accounts for about 40 percent of the water used in the United States.

● Satellite pictures can locate hidden water pools under the desert floor. Modern drilling equipment can then reach the water to create new oases.

▲ Oil flares send smoke plumes into the desert air.

▶ Plastic tunnels cover healthy desert crops. The tunnels prevent precious water from **evaporating** into the dry desert air. Continual evaporation may encourage salts to rise to the surface of the desert. These salts kill most plant life and poison the soil.

JEALOUS GOOMBLE-GUBBON

For thousands of years people have told stories about the world around them. Often these stories try to explain something that people do not really understand, like how the world began or where light comes from. This tale is told by the Aboriginal people of Australia.

Long ago in Australia was the Dream Time when everything was made. The land was made, with mountains, plains, and valleys full of all sorts of animals, birds, and plants. And the sea was made, full of whales, dolphins, and plants. But there were not yet any fish.

All the birds had been given wonderful and extraordinary voices: Crow croaked his rasping caw, Kookaburra laughed her hilarious chuckle, and the other birds sang in all their different voices. They sat singing in the trees and bushes all day long, because they were so happy.

When I say they all had wonderful and extraordinary voices, I am forgetting Goomble-Gubbon, the turkey. Goomble-Gubbon could only make a low bubbling noise in his throat, which sounded like this: "goomble gubbon, goomble gubbon." All the other birds thought Goomble-Gubbon's voice was a great joke, and they sang even more beautifully when he was around just to tease him.

Of course, they didn't really mean to be cruel. They were all so happy themselves that they did not realize how much they were hurting poor Goomble-Gubbon's feelings. They were very fond of him in spite of his bad-tempered ways.

Goomble-Gubbon did not find his voice funny. He thought it was terrible, and he was very jealous of all the other birds' voices. He tried everything he could to improve his voice, but nothing was any use. If only the other birds' voices were not so wonderful and extraordinary, his voice would not seem so terrible, he thought.

One day was worse than ever before. The other birds had been laughing at Goomble-Gubbon all morning, and he was tired of it. So he went off to visit his friend Lizard. Lizard never laughed at his voice. The two of them sat talking and telling stories until the sun began to set. Just then, Kookaburra flew into the branches of a nearby tree and began to laugh.

Now, Kookaburra could not help laughing. She laughed at everything, even at things that were not at all funny, and Goomble-Gubbon should have known this really. But he was fed up with being teased by all the other birds, and so he thought that Kookaburra had flown over and perched on that very branch just to laugh at him.

"What do you think you're laughing at?" he snapped angrily.

Kookaburra looked most surprised and flew off to tell the other birds about Goomble-Gubbon's strange behavior.

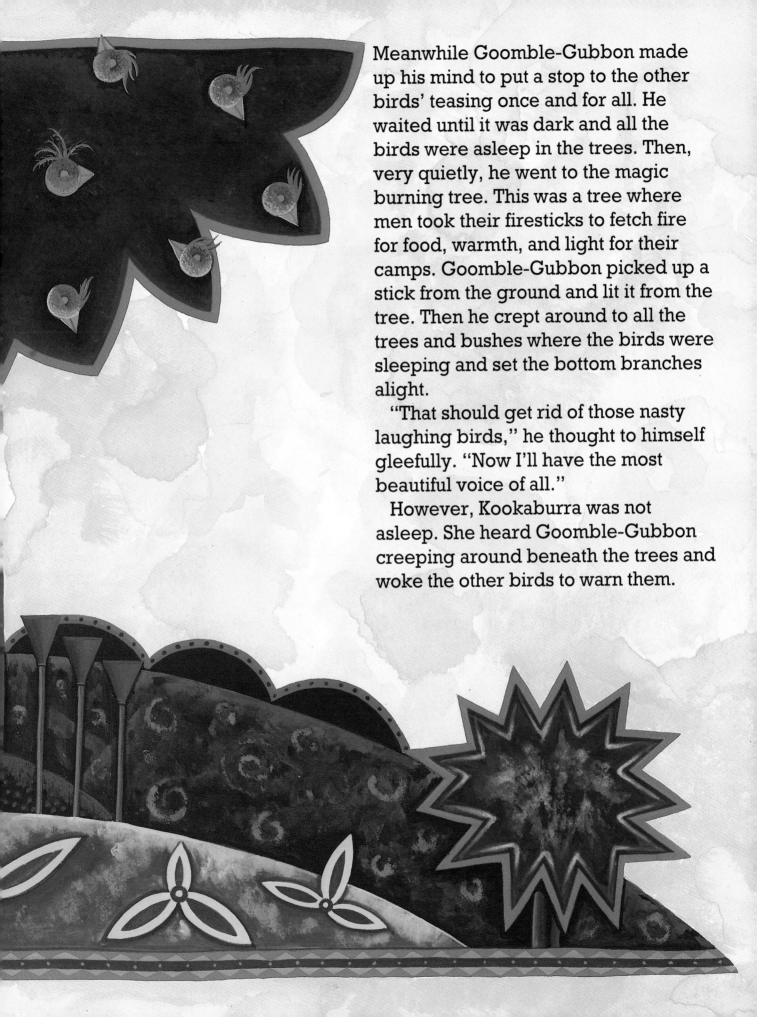

Meanwhile Goomble-Gubbon made up his mind to put a stop to the other birds' teasing once and for all. He waited until it was dark and all the birds were asleep in the trees. Then, very quietly, he went to the magic burning tree. This was a tree where men took their firesticks to fetch fire for food, warmth, and light for their camps. Goomble-Gubbon picked up a stick from the ground and lit it from the tree. Then he crept around to all the trees and bushes where the birds were sleeping and set the bottom branches alight.

"That should get rid of those nasty laughing birds," he thought to himself gleefully. "Now I'll have the most beautiful voice of all."

However, Kookaburra was not asleep. She heard Goomble-Gubbon creeping around beneath the trees and woke the other birds to warn them.

A great swarm of birds rose up from the trees, screeching and crying. The birds who could fly fast flew away as quickly as they could to far-off places where there was no fire. Those who could not fly fast enough to get away from the flames flew into the sea to cool off. As they entered the water, their wings turned into fins and their feathers became scales. At last there were fish in the sea!

Goomble-Gubbon was furious that his plan had not worked. He waved the firestick wildly, but he managed only to singe his own feathers a nasty smoky color and burn his head bright red too. He threw the firestick far out into the bush.

The fire in the trees went on burning until the land in the center of Australia was quite barren and dry. And that is how the desert came to be in the center of Australia. All because of jealous Goomble-Gubbon.

TRUE OR FALSE?

Which of these facts are true and which ones are false? If you have read this book carefully, you will know the answers.

1. All deserts are very hot.

2. Deserts receive no rain at all during the year.

3. The Gobi Desert is the largest desert in the world.

4. Nights in the desert are extremely cold.

5. Lush rain forests can lie alongside rain shadow deserts.

6. Saguaro cacti can grow close to 50 feet (15 meters) high.

7. The ears of the American cottontail rabbit act as radiators.

8. A camel's humps are used to store water.

9. The dromedary has two humps and a thick coat.

10. The Tuareg were once known as the pirates of the desert.

11. Many desert towns are built from mud bricks.

12. In 1988 thousands of large blue fish rained down on a British village during a bad storm.

GLOSSARY

● **Arid** land is parched soil with sparse vegetation. Little rain falls on this type of land and it is prone to desertification.

● **Bushmen** are people who live in desert lands such as in Africa or Australia. They drink little, as they obtain enough moisture from eating underground roots and desert melons.

● **Desert** is a place with little vegetation where less than 10 inches (25 centimeters) of rain falls each year.

● **Desertification** is the process by which dry areas of land on the edge of deserts suffer from drought and also become desert. If regular rainfall returns to the area, the new region of desert could recover.

● **Domesticated** animals are those which have been bred by humans over many generations to be tame and to provide products such as meat, milk, leather, and wool.

● **Drought** is a period when very little or no rain falls. Crops do not grow, water is scarce, and animals and humans find it hard to survive.

● **Ephemerals** are tiny plants that survive as seeds in dry conditions such as desert sands. They wait for a period of heavy rain and then burst into flower.

● **Evaporation** is when water turns into tiny droplets of vapor in the air. This process happens each morning to the dew that has fallen during the night in the hot desert.

● **Extinct** means that the last member of an animal or plant species has died out as a result of overhunting, a change in its habitat, or its failure to compete with a new animal or plant.

● **Famine** is a period when food is scarce and many people and animals starve and die. This usually takes place after wartime or after a drought, when crops have been unable to grow.

● **Fertile** land is that which is good for growing lush and healthy crops.

● **Hunter-gatherers** are people who live off the land by harvesting food from the plants and animals that live there. They are skillful in taking only what the land can survive without.

Irrigation is the method by which farmers water land that naturally tends to be dry. Water is often channeled over land through ditches or retained on land with a hard, resistant surface such as low walls.

Nomads are people who travel from one area to another either to take their herds of animals to fresh grazing or to escape severe weather such as cold or drought. They feed mainly on products from their herds and live in tents, which can easily be packed up and carried on the next journey.

Scrubland is territory where vegetation grows low and stunted.

Taproots are long, thin roots that push their way through the layers of stone beneath the sand. They help some desert trees find moisture during long periods of drought.

Topsoil is the uppermost and richest layer of earth where most plants grow. The desert lacks topsoil, which has dried out with lack of rain and has blown away.

Tubers are short, thick parts of underground stems of certain plants. They are covered in small bumps.

Tropic of Cancer and **Tropic of Capricorn** are imaginary lines at about 23°27″ north and south of the equator. Most deserts are found along these two lines.

INDEX

RESOURCES

Animals of the Desert, by Stephen Savage, 1997. This book tells about mammals, birds, reptiles, amphibians, and invertebrates who have adapted to harsh desert conditions.

Desert Babies, by Kathy Darling, 1997. Learn about the emu, caracal, and many other desert babies in this book.

Desert Life,
http://www.desertusa.com/life.html
This Web site is loaded with detailed information about desert plants, animals, and people in the American Southwest.

Desert Mammals, by Elaine Landau, 1997. This book introduces children ages 5-8 to animals that make their home in the deserts.

Interfact Deserts, by World Book, 1999. This CD-ROM and book work together to help students learn about deserts and the animals that live in them. The disk is full of interactive activities, puzzles, quizzes, games, and interesting facts. The book contains fascinating information highlighted with lots of full-color illustrations and photographs.

What Is a Desert?
http://www.desertusa.com/desert.html
This Web site provides a description of a desert ecosystem, with links to resources about deserts in the United States and Mexico.

What Is the Desert?
http://www.desertusa.com:80/desert.html
This Web site provides information on various deserts.